WILD-
FLOWERS

Wild

flowers

Wildflowers

A desert after rain suddenly full of life with a carpet of yellows, whites and oranges. Luscious red blooms lighting up a dark forest interior. Spring meadows alive with daisies, buttercups and myriad other flowers. Wildflowers are everywhere and they have the power to inspire us and capture our imaginations. They are symbols of love, happiness, beauty, remembrance, regeneration and much more besides.

The delicate forms of flowers seem to make us reflect on our own frailties and appreciate the beauty not only of the blooms themselves but also of other aspects of life. This beautiful book depicts watercolour paintings and other artworks of wildflowers together with quotes that cover everything from deep philosophical thoughts to more humorous offerings.

"*We have the most beautiful planet – the Rockies, the purple fields of the United States, the Lake District, the Pyrenees, the turquoise seas of the tropics.*"

– DAN AYKROYD

"Be still when you
have nothing to say;
when genuine passion
moves you, say what
you've got to say,
and say it hot."

– D.H. LAWRENCE

"Love speaks in flowers.
Truth requires thorns."

– LEIGH BARDUGO

"*I guess it's easy to dream about things that are abstract, or impossible.*"

– MELISSA KEIL

"*Love is like wildflowers;*
It's often found in the most
unlikely places."

– RALPH WALDO EMERSON

"I'm on fire when I'm singing,
I'm completely in character,
I use my sense memories, and
every syllable of it is meant.
It's a very special thing."

– SINÉAD O'CONNOR

"*The sweet small clumsy feet of April came into the ragged meadow of my soul.*"

– E.E. CUMMINGS

"All problems become smaller if you don't dodge them, but confront them. Touch a thistle timidly, and it pricks you; grasp it boldly, and its spines crumble."

– WILLIAM HALSEY

"*The rose does best as a rose.*
Lilies make the best lilies.
And look! You –
the best you around!"

– RUMI

"Wild roses are fairest,
and nature a better gardener
than art."

– LOUISA MAY ALCOTT

"*Forgiveness is the fragrance that the violet sheds on the heel that has crushed it.*"

– MARK TWAIN

"*It was not the thorn bending to the honeysuckles, but the honeysuckles embracing the thorn.*"

– EMILY BRONTË

"*Stronger than alcohol,*
vaster than poetry,
Ferment the freckled red
bitterness of love!"

– ARTHUR RIMBAUD

"I know a bank where
the wild thyme blows,
Where oxlips and the
nodding violet grows,
Quite over-canopied
with luscious woodbine,
With sweet musk-roses
and with eglantine."

– WILLIAM SHAKESPEARE

"A good character is the best tombstone. Those who loved you and were helped by you will remember you when forget-me-nots have withered. Carve your name on hearts, not on marble."

– CHARLES SPURGEON

"*After climbing a great hill,
one only finds that there are
many more hills to climb.*"

– NELSON MANDELA

"In Hollywood,
brides keep the bouquets
and throw away the groom."

– GROUCHO MARX

"*Red stimulates and excites your nerves, pulse rate and blood circulation, and lends energy to your entire system. When you are fatigued, lethargic or sluggish for any reason, red has an energising influence.*"

– TAE YUN KIM

"*There are some who can live without wild things, and some who cannot. For us of the minority, the opportunity to see geese is more important than television, and the chance to find a pasque-flower is a right as inalienable as free speech.*"

– ALDO LEOPOLD

"There's no need
for red-hot pokers.
Hell is ...
other people!"

– JEAN-PAUL SARTRE

"I have as much pink as you can have. I love to see other women in pink. It's good for every shade of skin and hair."

– EVELYN LAUDER

"I've never wanted to chuck my mortgage, drop the kids off at their grandparents' and run gloriously naked in fields of flax."

– LAUREN GROFF

"*The secret of happiness is variety, but the secret of variety, like the secret of all spices, is knowing when to use it.*"

– DANIEL GILBERT

"You can cut all the flowers but you cannot keep spring from coming."

– PABLO NERUDA

"*Blue thou art,*
intensely blue;
Flower, whence came
thy dazzling hue?"

– JAMES MONTGOMERY

"Through the dancing poppies stole a breeze, most softly lulling to my soul."

– JOHN KEATS

"*How does the Meadow
flower its bloom unfold?
Because the lovely little flower
is free down to its root,
and in that freedom bold.*"

– WILLIAM WORDSWORTH

"*Buttercups, bright
eyed and bold,
hold their chalices of gold
to catch the sunshine
and the dew.*"

– JULIA CAROLINE DORR

"In joy or sadness,
flowers are our
constant friends."

– OKAKURA KAKUZO

"Children in a family are like flowers in a bouquet: there's always one determined to face in an opposite direction from the way the arranger desires."

– MARCELENE COX

"Why should I be unhappy?
Every parcel of my being
is in full bloom."

– RUMI

"If all flowers wanted to be roses, nature would lose her springtime beauty and the fields would no longer be decked out with little wildflowers."

– THERESE OF LISIEUX

"*I'll wait for you
under the bluebells.
I'll be there always.*"

– KIM HARRISON

"Aspirin is so good for roses,
brandy for sweet peas,
and a squeeze of lemon-juice
for the fleshy flowers,
like begonias."

– GERALD DURRELL

"Over every mountain
there is a path,
although it may not
be seen from the valley."

– THEODORE ROETHKE

"It took me time to understand my water lilies. I had planted them for the pleasure of it; I grew them without ever thinking of painting them."

– CLAUDE MONET

"To embrace the whole world
in friendship is wisdom.
This wisdom is
not changeable
like the flowers that
bloom and fade."

– THIRUVALLUVAR

"This is the bush,
as Australian as gum trees,
white Australia's bush legend:
tough, adaptable,
battlers in hard times,
opportunists in good,
conquerors of a continent.
Eucalypts could almost
teach newcomers
how to be Australian."

– BILL GAMMAGE

"A lily or a rose
never pretends,
and its beauty is that
it is what it is."

– JIDDU KRISHNAMURTI

"Almost every person,
from childhood,
has been touched by
the untamed beauty of
wildflowers."

– CLAUDIA ALTA JOHNSON

"Silence is golden
when you can't think of
a good answer."

– MUHAMMAD ALI

"Where innocent
bright-eyes daisies are
With blades of grass between,
Each daisy stands up
like a star
Out of a sky of green."

– CHRISTINA ROSSETTI

"I will be the gladdest thing
under the sun!
I will touch a hundred flowers
and not pick one."

– EDNA ST. VINCENT MILLAY

"One of the most attractive things about the flowers is their beautiful reserve."

– HENRY DAVID THOREAU

"*Little things seem nothing,
but they give peace,
like those meadow flowers
which individually seem
odourless but all together
perfume the air.*"

– GEORGES BERNANOS

"From plants that
wake when others sleep,
from timid jasmine buds that
keep their odour to themselves
all day, but when the sunlight
dies away let the delicious
secret out to every breeze
that roams about."

– THOMAS MOORE

*"If you are lucky enough
to have lived in Paris as a
young man, then wherever
you go for the rest of your life
it stays with you, for Paris is
a moveable feast."*

– ERNEST HEMINGWAY

"Tread Lightly,
she is near,
Under the snow,
Speak gently,
she can hear,
The daisies grow."

– OSCAR WILDE

"Happiness, I have grasped, is a destination, like strawberry fields. Once you find the way in, there you are, and you'll never feel low again."

– RACHEL SIMON

"In the Spring a
livelier iris changes on
the burnish'd dove;
In the Spring a young
man's fancy lightly turns
to thoughts of love."

– ALFRED LORD TENNYSON

"There is a flower,
a little flower
With silver crest
and golden eye,
That welcomes
every changing hour,
And weathers every sky."

– JAMES MONTGOMERY

"There was an old man
with a beard,
who said: 'It is
just as I feared!
Two owls and a hen,
four larks and a wren
have all built their nests
in my beard'."

– EDWARD LEAR

"Ah, summer, what power you have to make us suffer and like it."

– RUSSELL BAKER

"You might think that after thousands of years of coming up too soon and getting

frozen, the crocus family would have had a little sense knocked into it."

– ROBERT BENCHLEY

"*The flower is the poetry of reproduction.*
It is an example of the eternal seductiveness of life."

– JEAN GIRAUDOUX

"The snowdrop and primrose our woodlands adorn, and violets bathe in the wet o' the morn."

– ROBERT BURNS

"*It will create an excitement that will sweep the country like wildflowers.*"

– SAMUEL GOLDWYN

"You never tire of the moor.
You cannot think
the wonderful secrets
which it contains.
It is so vast, and so barren,
and so mysterious."

– ARTHUR CONAN DOYLE

"With a few flowers
in my garden,
half a dozen pictures
and some books,
I live without envy."

– FÉLIX LOPE DE VEGA

"*If you have two
loaves of bread,
keep one to nourish the body,
but sell the other to buy
hyacinths for the soul.*"

– HERODOTUS

"To those whom the trees, the birds, the wildflowers represent only 'locked-up dollars' have never known or really seen these things."

– EDWIN WAY TEALE

Published in 2024 by Reed New Holland Publishers
Sydney

Level 1, 178 Fox Valley Road, Wahroonga, NSW 2076, Australia

newhollandpublishers.com

A record of this book is held at the National Library of Australia.

ISBN 978 1 92107 366 3

Managing Director: Fiona Schultz
Publisher and Project Editor: Simon Papps
Designer: Andrew Davies
Production Director: Arlene Gippert
Printed in China

10 9 8 7 6 5 4 3 2 1

OTHER TITLES BY REED NEW HOLLAND INCLUDE:

A Guide to Flowers and Plants of Tasmania (Sixth Edition)
Launceston Field Naturalists Club
ISBN 978 1 92554 692 7

A Photographic Guide to Wildflowers of Outback Australia
Denise Greig
ISBN 978 1 86436 805 5

A Photographic Guide to Wildflowers of South-eastern Australia
Denise Greig
ISBN 978 1 86436 806 2

Australian Native Plants (Seventh Edition)
John W. Wrigley and Murray Fagg
ISBN 978 1 92554 691 0

Native Plants of Northern Australia (New Edition)
John Brock
ISBN 978 1 92554 682 8

Reed Concise Guide: Wildflowers of Australia
Ken Stepnell
ISBN 978 1 92151 755 6

For details of these books and hundreds of other Natural History titles see
newhollandpublishers.com and follow ReedNewHolland and NewHollandPublishers on Facebook